A Collection

Of

Research Papers

and

Postings

Volume One

POL1000

The Politics of American Government

By G. C. Jones

Table of Contents

Introduction

This is a collection of research papers, and discussion postings that I have written for one of the college classes I have took online. This book will start off with the first research paper written for POL1000 the Politics of American Government, then be followed by the discussion postings for each unit or week of class.

Some units had one assignment and two discussion postings. Others had different combinations of each. Some units did not have an assignment and as such there will be no research paper for that unit, but there could possibly still be discussion postings that may or may not be included with this collection of research papers and discussions.

These research papers and discussion postings are collected here for information and educational purposes only. Each chapter will represent one unit or week of class.

Chapter One

The Articles of Confederation and the Constitution

The Articles of Confederation was really the first attempt at a Constitution in the United States. The Articles of Confederation created a loose confederation of sovereign states and a weak central government, leaving most of the power with the state governments. The need for a much stronger federal government soon became apparent and eventually led to the Constitutional Convention in 1787 and ultimately to the Constitution that the United States continues to utilize to this day.

"The Constitution was designed in part to provide for a limited government in which political power would be confined to proper uses. The framers wanted to ensure that the government they were creating would not itself be a threat to freedom. To this end, they confined the national government to expressly granted powers and also denied it certain specific powers. Other prohibitions on government were later added to the Constitution in the form of stated guarantees of individual liberties in the Bill of Rights. The most significant constitutional provision for limited government, however, was a separation of powers among the three branches. The powers given to each branch enable it to act as a check on the exercise of power by the other two, an arrangement that during the nation's history has in fact served as a barrier to abuses of power.

Since the adoption of the Constitution, the public gradually has assumed more direct control of its representatives, particularly through measures that affect the way officeholders are chosen. Presidential popular voting (linked to the Electoral College), direct election of senators, and primary elections are among the devices aimed at strengthening the majority's influence. These developments are rooted in the idea, deeply held by ordinary Americans, that the people must have substantial direct influence over their representatives if government is to serve their interests" (Patterson, 2017).

This paper will attempt to compare and contrast how the Articles of Confederation and the Constitution handled each of the following topics:

1. Legislative organization and powers.

"There were key differences between the two documents in the how they both codified the law. The Articles of Confederation established a unicameral legislature, as opposed to the eventual bicameral system created by the Constitution. Voting power was delegated to states based on committees (consisting of anywhere from two to seven people) and each state had one vote in the Articles of Confederation; the Constitution allowed for a single vote for each legislative representative (for each state, two Senators and a number of House representatives based on census population)" (Difference Between, 2018).

In the Articles the term of legislative office was just one year, whereas in the constitution it is two years for Representatives and six years for Senators. In the Articles the term limit was no more than three out of every six years and, in the Constitution, there was no term limits established. In the Articles of Confederation, the pay for politicians was made by their home state or the state they represented, and in the Constitution, they were to be paid by the centralized federal government. The chair of legislature in the Articles was the president of Congress, whereas in the Constitution it is the Speaker of the house of Representatives and the Vice-President is the President of Congress. The power to coin money in the Articles was given to the states and central government but the Constitution only gave that power to the Federal government. (Mount, 2010).

2. Executive and centralized powers.

In the Articles of Confederation there was no central power such as what we now know of as The President. In the Articles, each state had just as much power as any other state. "Under the Articles of Confederation, the national government had no judiciary and no independent executive. All authority was vested in the Congress, but it was largely a creature of the states. Each of the 13 states had one vote in Congress, and each state appointed its congressional representatives and paid their salary. Legislation could be enacted only if 9 of the 13 state delegations agreed to it" (Patterson, 2017).

The Constitution established what we commonly refer to as Federal control. It established a centralized power to govern over all the states. Under the Articles, each state was free to make laws as if they were their own country. The constitution did away with this and as such unified all states into one country instead of what appeared to be several small countries ruling themselves. But the founding fathers were careful to make sure that the centralized power of the federal government could not gain too much control. They created a system of checks and balances that divided the power between the three main branches of government so that each branch would keep the other two in check.

The Constitution allowed for a central head of the government or President to hold an office over the executive branch of government. This president was to be elected by the people to represent the interest of the people and the country as a whole. It is a role that is to guide and control the feelings and beliefs of all the people throughout the entire country, and to be one that is picked by the people and not the ones already in the government.

3. The judicial system.

In the Articles of Confederation there was basically no form of judicial or executive branch established. This was one of the problems that came with the Articles and helped to lay the groundwork that created the need and the establishment of the Constitution. It had no power to enforce laws and was very limited in what it could or could not do. The Constitution established the judicial branch of the government to establish and translate the laws of the land, and as such gave more power to the centralized form of government.

The Constitution established that "Judicial power rests with the Supreme Court and with lower federal courts, which are subject to checks by the other branches of the federal government. Congress is empowered to establish the size of the federal court system, to restrict the Supreme Court's appellate jurisdiction in some circumstances, and to impeach and remove federal judges from office. More important, Congress can rewrite legislation that the courts have misinterpreted and can initiate amendments when it disagrees with court rulings on constitutional issues.

The president has the power to appoint federal judges with the consent of the Senate and to pardon persons convicted in the courts. The president also is responsible for executing court decisions, a function that provides opportunities to influence the way rulings are carried out" (Patterson, 2017).

4. The adding of amendments.

In the Articles of Confederation in order for an amendment to be made it had to be agreed upon by all the states. If one state did not agree, then the amendment was not made. This in itself severely limited the power of the country to accept change. If changes could not be made, then the country would be doomed to failure. For example, the Articles had to establishment for the rights of the citizens, or Bill or Rights; in order for this to change and give a set of common civil rights to its citizens, all states would have to agree on those rights. Since this would be virtually impossible for all states to simply agree, the founding fathers decided to hold a meeting to address these and other issues. This meeting became to be known as The Constitutional Convention.

"The original intent of the Constitutional Convention was to discuss the emerging problems in the new nation and make changes to the Articles of Confederation to address those problems. Very quickly however, the delegates determined to set the Articles of Confederation aside and start fresh. The result of their work was the Constitution of the United States" (J.L.C., 2015).

The Constitution established that in order to make changes or amendments, only three-quarters of the states had to agree on the changes to be made. "It also enumerated the relationship of the Federal Government and the states. Most importantly, it established the Bill of Rights, the first ten amendments of the Constitution which laid out the foundation for the civil liberties we enjoy as American citizens" (Difference Between, 2018).

The Constitution also established a way for the amendments to be proposed and enforced in what is known as article V of the Constitution. "Some constitutional scholars believe that Article V, which sets forth the amendment process, is the key to the Constitution's success. It establishes a process where adding amendments is not too easy, which would make the Constitution more like statutory law and less permanent—but also not too difficult, which would make violent revolution more likely. A proposed amendment must pass a two-thirds vote in both houses of Congress, or if two-thirds of the state's petition Congress, a new constitutional convention can be called to consider amendments. In any event, three-fourths of the state legislatures must ratify the amendment for it to become a permanent part of the Constitution" (Monk, 2013).

The Constitution also allows a way that the states can call for amendments to be made by "a constitutional convention called for by two-thirds of the State legislatures. None of the 27 amendments to the Constitution have been proposed by constitutional convention" (Archives, 2016). This by no means states that it could not happen, just that it is possible to be done if the central form of government is not making the needed changes. In today's society it could be more probable now than ever before.

In short, the Articles of Confederation gave us a good starting point to establish basically what we wanted in a country and government. But it did not go into detail enough, nor did it give the government enough power to actually create a common form of rule and unity over the country. Once the founding fathers decided to have a meeting and look into the changes that were needed, they basically decided to start from scratch and simply re-write the entire document. This is when the formed the Constitution of The United states of America.

The Constitution was a groundbreaking document that changed the course of human history. It gave us the freedom and control that was required in order for this country to survive. It also helped to lay the groundwork for other countries to follow in our footsteps and create their own form of government for the people and for the freedom of everyone. This is why it starts off with, We the People…

First Discussion Posting

How did Madison define faction?

Madison defined faction as "a number of citizens, whether amounting to a majority or a minority of the whole, who are united and actuated by some common impulse of passion, or of interest, adversed to the rights of other citizens, or to the permanent and aggregate interests of the community" (Madison, 1787).

What did Madison argue was the cure to faction?

He basically stated that there are two ways to handle factions. One is to eliminate the cause, and the other is to control the effects, (Madison, 1787). I personally believe that the latter of the two is happening more and more in our current society, but that is just my opinion.

Why did Madison argue for an indirect government versus a direct government?

I believe that one of the main reasons is because they had just rid themselves of a direct government where the rules was decided by one person or king. With a republic, the government would be elected by the people. "A republic, by which I mean a government in which the scheme of representation takes place, opens a different prospect, and promises the cure for which we are seeking" (Madison, 1787).

Do you think factions exist in our government today? Why or why not?

Yes, without a doubt, factions do exist in our current society. One only has to watch an episode of the evening news to see factions at work. One of the most popular factions, or so it seems, was eating Tide laundry pods and snorting condoms just a few months ago and are now trying to control the gun laws for the entire nation. These young people are not in the government employment as of yet, but they will be in just a few short years.

In the government itself, there are factions of people that believe big pharma companies have out best interest in mind. But that could not be further from the truth. For every pill they describe, there is a more natural way to heal. A way that does not have the side effects of a pill or opioid. But they do not make money that way, so they convince people that the pill is the best way to go. In doing this, they heal nothing, but they do create a customer for life and as such they keep profits rolling in for life.

Second Discussion Posting

One of the most interesting stories I have recently seen in the news is the one about the FBI raiding the office of one of President Trump's lawyers. There is a story about this in The New York Times that can be found in this link, https://www.nytimes.com/2018/04/09/us/politics/fbi-raids-office-of-trumps-longtime-lawyer-michael-cohen.html.

They must have found some evidence during their investigation that led them to believe a crime had been committed, otherwise they would not have been there in the first place. Trump then goes on Twitter and states that he is thinking about firing the one in charge of the investigation. In my opinion, this is one of the things that Madison argued against when he stated "No man is allowed to be a judge in his own cause, because his interest would certainly bias his judgment, and, not improbably, corrupt his integrity" (Madison, 1787). Yet, if Trump is allowed to fire the one investigating his actions, he is doing just that, he is judging his own cause.

"In his tirade against the F.B.I., Mr. Trump mused about the possibility that he might soon fire Mr. Mueller. Last June, the president vented internally about wanting to fire Mr. Mueller, but was talked out of it" (Apuzzo, 2018). I understand that he is the POTUS but that title does not give him a free pass to act like a dictator and fire anyone that looks into his dealings. This is exactly what our founding fathers were trying to prevent.

Chapter Two

Overview of Federalism

Should the states within the greater United States be able to pass laws to legalize marijuana?

"Marijuana refers to the dried leaves, flowers, stems, and seeds from the Cannabis sativa or Cannabis Indica plant. The plant contains the mind-altering chemical THC and other similar compounds. Extracts can also be made from the cannabis plant (see "Marijuana Extracts").

Marijuana is the most commonly used illicit drug in the United States.1 Its use is widespread among young people. In 2015, more than 11 million young adults ages 18 to 25 used marijuana in the past year" (Drugabuse, 2018).

Marijuana is a plant that can be grown virtually anywhere. It has been around for many centuries and has commonly used for medicinal purposes for thousands of years. "The first record of the drug's medicinal use dates to 4000 B.C. The herb was used, for instance, as an anesthetic during surgery, and stories say it was even used by the Chinese Emperor Shen Nung in 2737 B.C." (Blaszczak-Boxe, 2014).

Whether or not each state should be allowed to legalize the use of marijuana has been the center of a debate that has went on for at least a decade. The federal government first started their war on weed back in the 1930's with their advertisement campaign commonly referred to a reefer madness. In this short film they convinced the general public that is someone used weed or marijuana they would go mad and their lives would be destroyed. Many people believed what they were told even though there was no solid evidence proving what they were told.

The same general public that believed this reefer madness campaign did not realize that they were already using marijuana extracts in some medicines for many years with positive results. It was also used to make sails for sailing ships, clothes, and ropes up until Dupont introduced nylon ropes. Once nylon was developed, companies like Dupont jumped on the bandwagon and helped to pave the way for making marijuana illegal so they could sell more nylon rope and increase profits.

"Marijuana was listed in the United States Pharmacopeia from 1850 until 1942 and was prescribed for various conditions including labor pains, nausea, and rheumatism. Its use as an intoxicant was also commonplace from the 1850s to the 1930s. A campaign conducted in the 1930s by the U.S. Federal Bureau of Narcotics (now the Bureau of Narcotics and Dangerous Drugs) sought to portray marijuana as a powerful, addicting substance that would lead users into narcotics addiction. It is still considered a "gateway" drug by some authorities. In the 1950s it was an accessory of the beat generation; in the 1960s it was used by college students and "hippies" and became a symbol of rebellion against authority" (Narconon, 2018).

When President Nixon enacted the Controlled Substance Act of 1970, they took the power away from the states to control the use and legalization of marijuana. They then classified marijuana as a serious narcotic. Listed alongside heroin and cocaine. Many people now know that marijuana is nowhere the serious narcotic as they previously mentioned drugs. We will probably never know exactly why it was classified in this manner, but it remains scheduled that way to this day.

Amendment 10 of the United States Constitution states "The powers not delegated to the United States by the Constitution, nor prohibited by it to the States, are reserved to the States" (Patterson, 2017). This amendment gives the states a reserve power, to control the laws of their land as they see fit. However, the federal government took their rights to control marijuana laws in 1970. Whether or not the states can take back this power remains to be seen and is a serious debate in our current health conscience society.

One of the main reasons for allowing the states to control the legalization of marijuana is the current opioid crisis. It is believed by many that if marijuana was legal it would help to curb opioid addiction and abuse. If people can be prescribed a plant-based product for their pain and other ailments, rather than be prescribed an opioid, it actually could be better and healthier for patients to use. After all, nobody in the history of humans has ever died from an overdose of marijuana.

"Contrary to popular belief, marijuana is not as addicting as one may think. Dr. Sanjay Gupta, CNN's Chief Medical Correspondent, recently wrote in his essay, "Why I Changed My Mind About Weed," that we have been "systematically misled" on marijuana. He reports that marijuana leads to dependence in around 9-10 percent of adult users. Cocaine hooks about 20 percent of its users, and heroin gets 25 percent of its users addicted. The worst culprit is tobacco, with 30 percent of its users becoming addicted" (Jacques, 2017).

Since every state has their own amount of opioid abuse and health problems, the right to determine how to treat patients should be in their hands instead of the federal government. If one state has a higher number of military veterans that are diagnosed with PTSD and need marijuana to naturally treat that symptom than a state that has very of these patients; then why should they be bound to the laws of a state that does not have the same problems? When the power is controlled by the federal government rather than in the states, then it is doing just that, not allowing each state to treat their own patients.

"Elvis Alonzo began smoking cannabis as a last resort. Three years in the Marine Corps and 13 years with the Glendale Police Department in Arizona—where he was exposed to murders, suicides and people dying in his arms—had left him emotionally crippled. Toward the end of his police service, doctors diagnosed Alonzo with post-traumatic stress disorder and prescribed various medications to temper his nightmares and flashbacks. The drugs "turned me into a zombie," he says. "I was so out of it that I couldn't even drive, so they (the police department) had to medically retire me." Alonzo stopped showering. His wife left him, and he nearly lost his house. Then a friend suggested he try marijuana to relieve his symptoms. "It's been a godsend," he says. "It curbs my anxiety, and it makes me sleep fantastic for at least four hours. It needs to be studied."

Thousands of military veterans have echoed Alonzo's claim for years. They have pressured federal and state legislators to legalize medicinal cannabis and ease rules on research into the plant's apparent therapeutic properties, arguing that it could help reduce suicide rates among former soldiers" (Serrano, 2018).

Another sound reason to allow the states to control the legalization of marijuana is for the money it can generate for each state, and also in turn for the federal government. "North American marijuana sales grew by an unprecedented 30% in 2016 to $6.7 billion as the legal market expands in the U.S. and Canada, according to a new report by Arcview Market Research.

North American sales are projected to top $20.2 billion by 2021 assuming a compound annual growth rate of 25%. The report includes Canada for the first time as it moves towards implementing legal adult use marijuana" (Borchardt, 2017). This is simple economic growth, all of which can be taxed and used to finance the government. Instead of having a deficit, it could be in the profit zone and no longer have any worries such as how to pay for schools, or road and bridge repairs.

It also seems to be one of the fastest growing industries that our country has ever seen in it's history. "To put this in perspective, this industry growth is larger and faster than even the dot-com era. During that time, GDP grew at a blistering pace of 22%. Thirty percent is an astounding number especially when you consider that the industry is in early stages.

Arcview's new editor-in-chief Tom Adams said, "The only consumer industry categories I've seen reach $5 billion in annual spending and then post anything like 25% compound annual growth in the next five years are cable television (19%) in the 1990's and the broadband internet (29%) in the 2000's."" (Borchardt, 2017).

The bottom line is that legalization would be good for everyone, the economy, the government, veterans, drug addicts, and the patients in the hospitals. If anyone understands why alcohol and cigarettes are legal, then they should have nothing to say about legalizing marijuana. Allowing each state to make these decisions sounds as simple as allowing each state to decide how old one has to be before they can obtain a driver's license or purchase alcohol and cigarettes.

They will allow each state to decide when one can take control of a car and risk a stranger's life in an auto accident that happened while they were texting and smoking a cigarette, but then they decide that the states should not have the power to legalize a medicine. When one says it that way it sounds totally preposterous? If it doesn't, it should and people should stop believing everything the stereotype would have people believe.

They will allow each state to decide how old one has to be before they can drink alcohol and ruin their lives, kidneys, home life, and their minds; but refuse to allow each state to decide whether or not they can legalize a plant that could also restore the farming industry just seems to not be a sane choice.

There are many people, in and out of politics, that truly believe that amendment ten of the Constitution gives the states the reserve power to make their own laws and regulations. But there are also many that see the Controlled Substance act of 1970 to be a display of the federal power to take away that reserve power from the states. In other words, the states have this power until the federal government decides to take it away from the states. This should be considered to be an abuse of power by the federal government.

If this power can be taken away from the states at any time, then they truly did not possess it in the first place. It is simply in their hands when the federal government lets it hang in limbo or doesn't decide on it. Once they decide to make that decision, it is no longer in the hands of the states, or in limbo. If it is truly a reserve power that the states possess, then it could not, and should not be taken away by the federal government.

Power was granted to the states so that the federal government could not become too powerful. It is designed to help keep the federal government in check. But once the power can be stripped from the states, the power to keep the federal government in check is taken away from the states. In order for the states to truly keep the government in check, this power should be granted back to the states. Keeping the federal government in check should be the main reason to allow each state to decide on the legalization of marijuana issue.

Therefore, the power to decide on marijuana is just a drop in the bucket. The main reason to allow each state to make these decisions should be to maintain order in the country itself and to keep the federal government in check. So that they do not become too powerful and end up being the type of government that people wanted to get away from when this country was founded and organized by our founding fathers, the writers of the United States Constitution.

First Discussion Posting

1. GMO labeling.

I believe that GMO labeling should be in government control. Simply because it is an issue that should have a standard set of rules for everyone. Since we have the FDA and the USDA that already controls items such as labeling. Allowing the federal government to regulate GMO labeling is just an addition to the rules already in place that are already being controlled by the federal government.

Everyone should already be aware that GMO foods are one of the reasons for many of the health problems humans are facing today. If each state was allowed to control GMO labeling it would be comparable to each of the states controlling the legalization of marijuana. The states that have made it legal have experienced many people trying to cross state borders with it. If each state was allowed to control GMO labeling, it would be a similar situation where GMO food was being transported into states that did not allow GMO foods.

2. Gun control.

It is my understanding that each state already has the power to create and regulate gun control. However, in today's society, many people are calling on the federal government to take charge of gun control. One thing most of those people do not realize is that there actually are federal gun control laws, but they mainly are just to regulate interstate transfer of guns.

"The Federal Firearms Act of 1938 ("FFA") imposed a federal license requirement on gun manufacturers, importers, and those persons in the business of selling firearms. The term federal firearms licensee ("FFL") is commonly used today to refer to the members of the gun industry on whom this license requirement is imposed. In addition to the licensing component of the FFA, the Act required licensees to maintain customer records and made illegal the transfer of firearms to certain classes of persons, such as convicted felons. These classes of persons are commonly referred to as "prohibited purchasers." The circumstances resulting in the prohibition (such as a felony conviction) are often referred to as "disabilities." The FFA was repealed by the Gun Control Act of 1968. However, many of its provisions were reenacted as part of the subsequent act" (Giffords, 2017).

If a criminal wants a gun, there are no amount of laws that will stop them from getting a gun. Laws only affect the people that are willing to obey the law. If one state decides to outlaw all guns, then someone wanting to commit a crime will simply go across state lines to get the gun. In order for a law to have any effect on criminals, all guns would have to be outlawed in every state (and we all know that is NOT going to happen) and even then, it would not be 100%effective.

If one wanted to stop guns from being used in a crime, then the only way to do that would be to start executing everyone that used a gun in a crime regardless of what the crime was or how minor the crime was. This would curb gun violence just like hanging someone from a rope stopped many people from stealing horses in the old west.

Second Discussion Posting

"The United States and European allies launched airstrikes on Friday night against Syrian research, storage and military targets as President Trump sought to punish President Bashar al-Assad for a suspected chemical attack near Damascus last weekend that killed more than 40 people.

Britain and France joined the United States in the strikes in a coordinated operation that was intended to show Western resolve in the face of what the leaders of the three nations called persistent violations of international law. Mr. Trump characterized it as the beginning of a sustained effort to force Mr. Assad to stop using banned weapons, but only ordered a limited, one-night operation that hit three targets" (Cooper, Gibbons-Neff, and Hubbard, 2018).

This just goes to give us an example of why a federal government is needed, or Federalism. Can you imagine if there were no federalism or federal government? How would that work in a situation like the article I mentioned? Would all states be able to help coordinate an airstrike like this? Probably not, it would still be in the planning and organizing stage of the process. The other countries would not have been able to work with that many separate governments to get the job done.

One more thing about having a strong federal government is that if there were none, countries like Syria and Russia would be able to take over the country by simply taking control of one state at a time. Just like the Germans did in World War II when they rolled through one country at a time, so would others do to the United States if federalism did not exist in our current society.

Chapter Three

Voting Rights and Participation

"Equality has always been the least developed of America's founding concepts. Not even Thomas Jefferson, who wrote the words, believed that a precise meaning could be given to the claim of the Declaration of Independence that "all men are created equal." Nevertheless, the promise contained in that phrase has placed history on the side of those seeking greater equality. Every civil rights movement, from suffrage for males without property in the 1830s to LGBT rights today, has derived moral strength from the nation's pledge of equality for all.

Nevertheless, America's history reveals that disadvantaged groups have never achieved greater equality without a struggle. The policies that protect these groups today are the result of sustained political action that forced entrenched interests to relinquish or share their privileged status" (Patterson, 2017).

The Voting Rights Act of 1965 was written to end the social in-justice that had been facing the African-American population for decades. Even though blacks had been given the right to vote in 1870, very few were actually being allowed to vote. Some areas would not allow them to vote if they could not read and write, other areas would make up bogus rules in order to keep them from voting. Some areas even required an African-American to recite the entire United States Constitution before being allowed to vote in an election. Without proper federal over-sight, the conditions could not be changed throughout all the states.

The attack on peaceful marchers by state troopers in 1965 in Selma Alabama showed the country that major changes had to be made to end civil and voting rights discrimination in America. "Congress determined that the existing federal anti-discrimination laws were not sufficient to overcome the resistance by state officials to enforcement of the 15th Amendment. The legislative hearings showed that the Department of Justice's efforts to eliminate discriminatory election practices by litigation on a case-by-case basis had been unsuccessful in opening up the registration process; as soon as one discriminatory practice or procedure was proven to be unconstitutional and enjoined, a new one would be substituted in its place and litigation would have to commence anew" (DOJ, 2017).

"The Voting Rights Act of 1965, signed into law by President Lyndon B. Johnson, aimed to overcome legal barriers at the state and local levels that prevented African Americans from exercising their right to vote as guaranteed under the 15th Amendment to the U.S. Constitution. The Voting Rights Act is considered one of the most far-reaching pieces of civil rights legislation in U.S. history" (History, 2009).

Once the Voting Rights Act of 1965 was passed, it had one of the most significant effects on voting in America that has ever been experienced. No longer could African-Americans be kept from the voting polls during an election. No longer would they be facing white only voting precincts or be required to recite the entire constitution to vote. "The Voting Rights Act had an immediate impact on black participation. In the ensuing presidential election, black turnout in the South jumped by 20 percentage points" (Patterson, 2017).

The Voting Rights Act of 1965 did not come without its complications and challenges. Some states that felt the way the federal level determined who and where would get the federal over-sight was unfair and they challenged it in court. Due to these challenges the act is constantly under scrutiny and being changed or adapted to fit modern society requirements. One of the most notable challenges came in 2013 with the Supreme court decision in Shelby County vs. Holder.

"Congress has regularly renewed the Voting Rights Act, but the Supreme Court by a 5–4 vote in Shelby County v. Holder (2013) invalidated the provision (Section 4) of the Voting Rights Act that included the formula for determining which states and counties were subject to federal oversight. The formula included factors such as an area's use of tests or requirements aimed at restricting minority participation. Designated states and counties were required by the preclearance provision (Section 5) of the Voting Rights Act to obtain permission from federal officials before they made changes—such as redrawing electoral districts or altering registration requirements—that might adversely affect a minority group. In its Shelby County decision, the Court's majority held that the formula for identifying the states and counties subject to federal oversight was based on "obsolete statistics" and could not be applied unless Congress updated it" (Patterson, 2017).

The Voting Rights Act of 1965 has been amended five times over the last few decades in an attempt to keep up with the changes in modern society. The amendments in 1970 and 1975 only changed section five of the act. The amendments in 1982 only affected section four of the act. The last change to the act was made in 2006. "Congress renewed the special provisions of the Act in 2006 as part of the Fannie Lou Hamer, Rosa Parks, Coretta Scott King, Cesar E. Chavez, Barbara Jordan, William Velazquez and Dr. Hector Garcia Voting Rights Act Reauthorization and Amendments Act. The 2006 legislation eliminated the provision for voting examiners" (DOJ, 2017).

"Some states had moved to tighten access to voting by imposing restrictions, hoping to force an overturning of key parts of the original law in the courts, which is what happened. The Washington Post reports that since 2010, 21 states have passed new laws restricting voting access. Some cut back on early voting hours and others limited the number of documents considered valid to identify a legitimate voter. This process of backlash intensified since the high court decision in 2013. For 14 states, the 2016 presidential election will be first to be held under their new restrictions. (On the other hand, some states and the District of Columbia have implemented more lenient policies that encourage the casting of ballots, such as offering early voting without citizens having to offer an excuse.)

Keeping the issue alive is the movement in Congress to strengthen the original voting rights law. "It's important to fix a decision of the United States Supreme Court and make it easier, make it simple for all of our people to participate in a democratic process," said Rep. John Lewis, D-Ga., sponsor of a new voting rights bill and a pioneer of the civil rights movement since the 1960s" (Walsh, 2015).

More and more in today's political society we are hearing about voters' rights partially because of all the accusations that have been said during recent presidential elections. We hear about people voting that are not supposed to be voting, and most recently we are hearing that other countries are interfering in our voting system. Investigations are currently under way to determine if there are any truths to these stories and accusations. However, just like past conspiracy stories about our federal government, we might not know the truth for decades to come if we ever are allowed to know.

This alone is one of the main reasons more people need to get out to vote. Voter rights are very important to ensure that everyone gets a fair and equal chance to vote in any election. The more people that turn out to vote can help to decrease the odds of corruption from happening. When people vote, they are making their voice heard through that vote. When they are not allowed to make that voice heard, then they are being suppressed. The Voting Rights Act of 1965 is designed to end suppression of voters.

After all, it is the squeakiest wheel that gets grease. Our vote is our squeak and we cannot grease the wheels of justice without making a little squeak.

First Discussion Posting

"Sen. Ron Wyden and Rep Earl Blumenauer, both Democrats from Oregon, introduced a bill that would expand their state's vote-by-mail system to the entire country. The bill has little chance of passage — one of the core truths of US politics is that anything that increases voting turnout hurts Republicans, so they inevitably oppose it" (Roberts, 2017). This statement alone shows that voting by mail would increase voter turnout.

Voter turnout has increased in Oregon more from 2012 to 2016 than in any other state (McElwee, Schaffner, and Rhodes, 2017). "Washington state's 2008 General Election broke a voter turnout record that had stood since World War II" (Wyman, 2008). This shows that voting by mail has increased voter turnout in both of these states. Here in Kentucky where voting by mail, or absentee voting is limited, studies have shown that voter turnout is decreasing, especially among people with disabilities (Henderson, 2017). "Tennessee ranks 40th in the nation in voter registration and last in voter turnout. More than 838,000 adult Tennesseans are not registered to vote" (Buie, 2017).

I believe voting by mail would be a good idea for all states. It would increase voter turnout, and hopefully go along ways towards ending voter fraud. If more people turned out to vote, we could hopefully eliminate government abuse by career politicians. I personally believe that career politicians are one of the big problems in our current form of government. When someone has been in office for more than ten years, they lose touch with the people they are supposed to represent.

Stopping voter fraud in another main concern in today's world, or at least that is what the television news programs are supposed to tell us all. "Mail-based voting systems today are far less risky than most polling place elections, precisely because they distribute ballots (and electoral risk) in such a decentralized way. To have any reasonable chance of success, an organized effort to defraud a mail-based system and its safeguards must involve hundreds (if not thousands) of separate acts, all of them individual felonies, that must both occur and go undetected to have any chance of success" (Roberts, 2017).

I personally have stopped voting because I have lost faith in our current system. I do not believe that my vote actually does any good in our modern-day elections.

Second Discussion Posting

"Colorado's Supreme Court on Monday knocked six-term U.S. Rep. Doug Lamborn from his party's primary, saying the Colorado Springs Republican didn't collect enough valid voter signatures to qualify for the ballot.

The court reversed a lower court ruling in a lawsuit that challenged the validity of voter signatures that Lamborn's campaign tried to use to make the June 26 primary.

The court ruled that Lamborn fell 58 signatures short of the 1,000 from registered Republicans he needs to qualify for the primary ballot because two of the people who circulated petitions for Lamborn were not legal Colorado residents" (Anderson, Riccardi, 2018).

In my opinion, if this guy used signatures from people that were not registered to vote in his area, then he should not be allowed to ever run for any office. Hopefully if more states turn to voting by mail this kind of problem can be eliminated. If he can't use people from his area, then is he truly representing the people of his area?

I realize that he just used people passing around the petitions that were not from his area, but it also shows that with fewer people voting, there is a smaller crowd to convince about which way to vote. If more people turned out to vote because of voting by mail, people having this type of influence and interaction could seriously slow down. If voter registration increases, the people would have more power to control what their government actually does.

Chapter Four

Political Parties

"A strong majority of millennials — 71 percent — say the Republican and Democratic parties do such a poor job of representing the American people that a third major party is needed, according to the results of a new NBC News/GenForward poll.

Sixty-three percent of millennials disapprove of the way President Donald Trump is handling his job as president. But millennials also hold a variety of political institutions in poor regard, and 65 percent think the country is on the wrong track overall" (Hartig, and Perry, 2017).

In this research paper we will delve into the political party world of politics. We will examine three political parties, the Democratic party, the Republican party, and one third-party commonly known as the Libertarian party. We will look into their views on two subjects such as abortion and the death penalty.

"The Democratic Party strongly and unequivocally supports Roe v. Wade and a woman's right to make decisions regarding her pregnancy, including a safe and legal abortion, regardless of ability to pay. We oppose any and all efforts to weaken or undermine that right. Abortion is an intensely personal decision between a woman, her family, her doctor, and her clergy; there is no place for politicians or government to get in the way. We also recognize that health care and education help reduce the number of unintended pregnancies and thereby also reduce the need for abortions. We strongly and unequivocally support a woman's decision to have a child by providing affordable health care and ensuring the availability of and access to programs that help women during pregnancy and after the birth of a child, including caring adoption programs" (DPP, 2012).

The Republican Party does not support abortion. They believe the right to live for an unborn child is secured by the United States Constitution and the Fourteenth Amendment. They believe that public funds should not be used for healthcare and that includes the issue of abortion. They want their party to support traditional family values and they try to select and support judges that will also support those same beliefs, (RPP, 2012). They even go as far as stating that they believe the right to have an abortion should be banned altogether.

The Libertarian Party believes that the right to choose should not be allowed to be made by the government, (LPP, 2012). This in itself shows that they do believe in the right to have an abortion but do not want to come right out and say so. They seem to believe that if they openly support abortion, they will be too much like the Democratic Party on the issue of abortion. Since they want to separate themselves from that and any other party, they have to word their answer differently so they appear to have their own opinion.

The Democratic Party does state that they believe the death penalty should not be arbitrary. This does not openly support the death penalty because it is basically saying that the death penalty is needed in some cases, but that it should be certain that it is needed. They want to support DNA testing to ensure that the correct person is executed. They also admit that there are inequalities in the current form of the justice system and that these issues need to be addressed, (DPP, 2012).

The Republican Party believes that criminals cannot harm anyone if they are behind bars. They believe in many cases that the maximum penalty should be enforced especially when gangs, or when violent crimes are committed. They also believe that the penalty for drug dealers, rape, or any sexual offense should be stricter than they currently are. They want judges to be able to impose the death penalty whenever they see fit to do so.

"Liberals do not understand this simple axiom: criminals behind bars cannot harm the general public. To that end, we support mandatory prison sentencing for gang crimes, violent or sexual offenses against children, repeat drug dealers, rape, robbery and murder. We support a national registry for convicted child murderers. We oppose parole for dangerous or repeat felons. Courts should have the option of imposing the death penalty in capital murder cases" (RPP, 2012).

The Libertarian Party believes that there should be stricter punishments for crimes but they do not believe that there should be a death penalty, (LPP, 2012). This seems to contradict itself in the fact that how can they believe there should be strict punishments but no death penalty? They simply state that they believe stricter punishment reduces crime, they support restitution, more rights for anyone accused, the three strikes rule has failed the system, and so has the enforcement of the death penalty, (LPP, 2012).

In summary, the Democrats support abortion, the Republicans do not support abortion and believe it should be banned altogether, and the Libertarians believe that abortion is needed in society but that the government should not be the ones making that decision. So basically, the Democrats agree on abortion and openly support the right to choose, and the Republicans do not support it in any way.

The Democratic party supports the death penalty when it has been fully and without doubt that it is needed to make the world a better place to live for everyone else. The Republicans believe that the death penalty should be an option in more criminal cases than it is currently used to reduce the crime rate. And the Libertarians believe that the death penalty should not exist, but they do want to enforce stricter penalties. Stricter penalties would drastically increase the cost of housing inmates in the criminal system, they have not been seen addressing this part of the issue.

In today's world, especially with all the collusion and corruption that is currently happening with President Trump's administration, people are simply losing faith in either of the two major parties. They believe it is time for major changes to be made in our political system. This fact alone is why the third-party candidates are gaining ground in the political world.

As it was stated earlier in this research paper, many of the younger generations do not believe that either party has their best interest in mind. This will lead them to a third-party choice in politics, even if they do not see eye to eye on several issues, they will choose a third-party over either the Democratic Party or the Republican Party.

Over the next decade, it is very possible that both the Democrats and the Republicans could be taken out of the equation when it comes to majority rule in politics. Many people that previously supported their party faithfully are now doubting their choices in our last Presidential election.

"Many American union workers who voted for President Donald Trump in the 2016 election are increasingly beginning to regret their decision—and realize that Trump has been firmly on the side of the rich all along.

That's according to new survey data published by Reuters on Friday, which shows that between March of 2017 and March of this year, Trump's support among union members has fallen by 15 percent" (Johnson, 2018).

This shows a major shift in what the people believe about their politicians. They are tired of being lied to, and they are tired of politicians that will tell them anything with no intent on doing what is right. This in itself will lead to a major shift in American politics over the next decade towards third parties.

"After the Civil War, the nation settled into the pattern of competition between the Republican and Democratic parties that has lasted through today. The durability of the two parties is due not to their ideological consistency but to their ability to change during periods of crisis. By abandoning at these crucial times their old ways of doing things, the Republican and Democratic parties have reorganized themselves—with new bases of support, new policies, and new public philosophies.

These periods of extraordinary party change are known as party realignments. A realignment typically involves three basic elements:

The emergence of unusually powerful and divisive issues

An election contest or contests in which the voters shift their partisan support

An enduring change in the parties' policies and coalitions

Realignments are rare. They do not occur simply because one party takes control of government from the other in a single election. Realignments result in deep and lasting changes in the party system that affect subsequent elections as well. By this standard, there have been four realignments since the 1850s" (Patterson, 2017).

I believe that in America today there is a change in politics happening. During the last presidential election, there were many people that did not vote along their usual party lines. Many people did not want to vote their usual Democrat because of Hillary, and many people did not want to vote their usual Republican because of Trump. I believe that this alone shows a shift in alignment of the political parties.

One advantage of having a third party is that it gives the people more choices of candidates to vote for in an election. Another advantage is that they can help to separate candidates when the Republican and Democratic parties seem to have similar platforms.

One dis-advantage is that a third party can split the votes. If one party loses votes to a third party, it can result in an easy win for the other party. Another dis-advantage is with the electoral college. "If a third-party candidate were to win a number of states in a presidential election it may result in no candidate winning a majority of electoral votes after the election. If this happened, one candidate may tell his electoral college voters to vote for another candidate, or the House of Representatives may vote for the president. Another option could be a run-off, or special election, which would take additional time and money" (Carpenter, 2017).

Second Discussion Posting

"In one wing of the GOP, Republicans say they support President Donald Trump more than the party itself, while those in the other wing back the party more than they do Mr. Trump. People in both groups of our WSJ/NBC News poll voted for the president in 2016. The two groups split on a host of issues — race, immigration, trade, Mr. Trump's use of Twitter, views of the FBI — though they seem to agree on lowering taxes. This is all laid out in a new in-depth graphic by Aaron Zitner and Gabriel Gianordoli.

On the Democratic side, opposition to Mr. Trump has partially masked a set of conflicts within the Democratic Party. Tensions over health care, trade and other issues have intensified as the party's liberal wing has gained power, and they are turning up during this year's primary

elections" (Jamerson, 2018).

This just shows that there are changes being made to each party and how Americans are

feeling about the typical two-party system. With all the controversy and lies being told to the

public by politicians, changes need to be made to the system. Politicians need to be held to the

same set of rules that are applied to the general public.

Chapter Five

First Discussion Posting

The group I chose is the Council for Citizens Against Government Waste. "Council for Citizens Against Government Waste's mission is to advocate the elimination of waste and inefficiency in government through lobbying and grassroots activities. Each year, CCAGW tabulates its Congressional Ratings, evaluating how each member of Congress measures up on key tax and spending votes...Citizens Against Government Waste's mission is to eliminate waste, mismanagement, and inefficiency in the federal government" (CCAGW, 2018).

Their website can be found on the Internet at http://www.ccagw.org/

One way this group has sought to influence policy is by posting a 'porker of the month' award to the politician that has demonstrated blatant disregard for the best interest of the public or taxpayers. This puts a politician in the spotlight and lets everyone know about their actions that were not in the best interest of the country.

Another way they try to influence policy is with their congressional ratings for politicians. They rate each one in Congress and that rating lets the people know which way they voted on policies and if their vote was in the best interest of the people.

I am not sure if this group actually has made a difference, but I would like to think they have. Everyone nowadays is aware that the government waste a lot of money. It seems to be a commonly known fact, but nobody does anything about it. I would personally like to see this group get a bigger voice in the ear of the American people. If more people knew exactly how much corruption takes place, then they would be more likely to stand up and say no to the corrupt politicians.

Second Discussion Posting

"Republican mega donor Sheldon Adelson gave a $30 million check to the Congressional Leadership Fund, Politico reported on Thursday.

House Speaker Paul D. Ryan flew to Las Vegas, where Mr. Adelson resides, in order to meet with him, but as an elected official he is not allowed to ask for a seven-figure sum. Former Minnesota Sen. Norm Coleman, who heads the Republican Jewish Coalition, asked Mr. Adelson for the contribution, according to Politico.

The check is larger than his 2016 donation and comes much earlier in the campaign cycle, showing Republicans aren't taking any chances when it comes to maintaining control of the House" (Persons, 2018).

This is the type of special interest groups that we all have become accustomed to hearing about. We here about it so much that we no longer see anything wrong with it. It is one of the main contributors to our corrupt society. It gives an edge to one group over another and is based on nothing but greed. If things were done fairly, this guy would have to give the same amount to all parties, or shut up and keep his money in his pocket.

Chapter Six

Budget Simulation

1. How easy or difficult was it to balance the budget?

I actually found it easy to cut the budget, and it would have been easier to accomplish if the payroll of all politicians and their pensions were on the line to be cut.

2. How did you feel about the choices you had to make to balance the budget? Why did you make the choices you made?

I feel good about the choices I made to cut the budget. I believe that there were some areas that should have been allowed to be cut even more. Most of the cuts I made were influenced by corruption and dishonesty that I have seen in each particular area, so in some ways the cuts I made were a form of punishment to that area.

For example, in the area of International Affairs I made the maximum cuts that were possible because we need to take care of ourselves before we attempt to take care of other countries. Most of our politicians would not have done this since they do not have intentions of taking care of the American people like they should be doing. As everyone is now finding out, many of those people making the decision to send money to other countries have business deals going on with that same country.

Food aid to other countries was cut to the max because we should not be giving food to other countries when we have so many people doing without food in our country. Funding for other countries military was also cut to the max since many of those countries or armies that we have funded end up turning on us. Some of the most extreme terrorist groups were originally funded by us and now they are trying to use their forces to harm us, so that should stop altogether immediately.

Funding for refugees should also stop so I made the maximum cuts available to that area as well. The government that made them refugees should be sent the bill for the cost of the refugees they made. If they refuse, drop a couple of bombs on their headquarters and see if they change their mind and pay the bill so they can continue without us reminding them to pay.

Cuts to the EPA were maxed out as well because when it comes to chemical spills and other harmful activities to the environment, the companies responsible for the accident should pay the bill. They make billions a year in profits but then have the federal government pay the bill for the cleanup because they also have politicians in their pocket that will vote to do so.

Cuts to the Space agency should also be maxed out until they tell us the truth about what they are actually doing. They should be required to inform the general public about what they are doing and what they have found in space. If aliens exist then they should tell us. If they found a spaceship and have been reverse engineering it since the 1940's then they should tell us. If there are military bases on the moon then they should let us know.

If we as a people and a country are supposed to trust our politicians and government officials, and agencies; then they should be honest with us. If someone's spouse is making dinner and we ask what is being cooked and they lie to us; should we trust them to tell us the truth about dinner tomorrow? The answer is no we should not, but we as a country have been mentally trained to believe whatever is told to us by our government, only to have them later prove they only had their own best interest in mind.

3. Although the numbers were different from the actual budget numbers, the activity
    resembled the types of choices that members of Congress have to make in order to
    balance the budget. What do you think are the chances that Congress would succeed at
    balancing the budget? Provide specific reasons drawn from your experience with the
    simulation.

I personally believe that the chances of Congress balancing the budget are slim to none. They simply are concentrating too much on their own needs given to them by the highest campaign contributor or their own wallet.

Recently there was a news story where one politician stated that rocks falling into the oceans were the cause of the ocean levels rising. With this type of intelligence, or lack of, should we wonder why the budget and the country is in such disarray? This Republican lawmaker is on the House Science, Space and Technology committee, REALLY? How can someone that obviously lacks enough intelligence to see what is wrong with his statement actually be in charge of anything but where to stop for lunch?

When we put people like that in charge of anything, we should expect the budget to not get balanced. How do we know he will not blame the economic problems on the rocks falling by themselves instead of allowing workers to push them into the ocean? Maybe he will also blame the poor road and bridge conditions in our country on people driving too fast over them.

He would have had a better chance of blaming the rise in ocean levels on plate tectonics, or the Earth's plates shifting. But instead he went above and beyond to show us all exactly how much trouble he has simply understanding the reality around us. Yet we expect this same person to help balance our nation's budget. Therefore, I am surprised if a budget gets balanced at all.

If we should expect Congress to balance the budget, then there should be no limitations on how much and where cuts actually need to be made. They will take money from Social Security and teachers pensions to balance the budget but they will not allow their own pensions to be cut along the way.

Recently there was another story in the news where a politician wanted to raise their pensions because he simply could not live on $175,000 a year. But at the same time, he expects a disabled veteran to live on $9,000 a year. I use this number because that is my income for one year.

We should not expect greedy people like this to be competent of balancing the nation's budget. When he requires to be above the people he represents, he is not doing the budget or the people justice. When a cowardly security guard that ran from a school shooting scene gets a retirement pension that is over four times what they expect me to live on; why should we expect anything less than an un-balanced budget.

First Discussion Posting

"U.S. Representative Thomas Massie entered Congress in November 2012 after serving as Lewis County Judge Executive. He represents Kentucky's 4th Congressional District which stretches across Northern Kentucky and 280 miles of the Ohio River.

U.S. Representative Massie attended the Massachusetts Institute of Technology where he earned a Bachelor's degree in Electrical Engineering and a Master's Degree in Mechanical Engineering. During school, he invented a technology that enabled people to interact with computers using their sense of touch, and leveraged that technology to found SensAble Technologies, Inc., which raised over $32 million of venture capital, created 70 jobs, and obtained 24 patents. The hardware and software he developed is now used to design automobiles, jewelry, shoes, dental prosthetics, and even reconstructive implants for wounded soldiers" (Massie, 2018).

Representative Massie introduced a bill that would end the federal department of education. He believes that the federal government should not decide what our children should or should not learn in schools.

Personally, I am not happy with Massie's work in the government. If he had any idea just how ignorant the people of this county really are, then he would not try to end the department of education. The fact that he would even try to end the department of education shows he is out of touch with the people of this county and does not have their best interest in mind.

Second Discussion Posting

"Former Secretary of State Rex Tillerson argued Wednesday that the U.S. is experiencing a "growing crisis of integrity and ethics" in his first public speech since leaving the Trump administration almost two months ago.

"When we as people, a free people, go wobbly on the truth even on what may seem the most trivial of matters, we go wobbly on America," Tillerson told the graduating class of cadets at the Virginia Military Institute.

While he did not mention President Trump by name, Tillerson did reference an "accepting of alternate realities" and warned that the country is in danger if Americans can't agree on basic facts.

"If our leaders seek to conceal the truth and we as people become accepting of alternative realities that are no longer grounded in facts, then as an American people we are on a pathway to relinquishing our freedom," Tillerson said" (Atwood, 2018).

I had to do a double take when I see this story because there are many people that truly believe that there has been an absence of ethics in politics for many years. Another thing that I find humorous about this story is that he had to problems with the lack of ethics until he was not part of the political machine. Why wasn't he saying this when he held a political position?

Chapter Seven

The Electoral College

"The delegates to the constitutional convention of 1787 feared that popular election of the president would make the office too powerful and accordingly devised an electoral vote system (the so-called Electoral College). The president was to be chosen by electors picked by the states, with each state entitled to one elector for each of its members of Congress (House and Senate combined). This system was modified after the election in 1828 of Andrew Jackson, who believed that the people's will had been thwarted four years earlier when he got the most popular votes but failed to receive an electoral majority. Although Jackson failed to persuade Congress to pass a constitutional amendment to eliminate the Electoral College, he prodded the states to tie their electoral votes to the popular vote outcome in the state. Under Jackson's reform, which is still in effect today, the candidate who wins a state's popular vote is awarded its electoral votes (see Chapter 2). Thus, the popular vote for the candidates directly affects their electoral vote, and one candidate is likely to win both forms of the presidential vote. Since Jackson's time, Rutherford B. Hayes (in 1876), Benjamin Harrison (in 1888), George W. Bush (in 2000), and Donald Trump (2016) have won the presidency after having lost the national popular vote" (Patterson, 2017).

Defining the electoral college

Merriam-Webster defines the electoral college as "a group of people chosen from each U.S. state who meet to elect the President and Vice President of the U.S. based on the votes of all the people in each state" (Merriam-Webster, 2018). What they do not tell you is that this group of people are newly elected for each Presidential election, and that they only meet once to vote then they are disbanded. The definition also does not tell you that they are supposed to be elected by the people to represent the popular vote.

Describing the role of the electoral college in the election of the president and vice president of the United States

The electoral College is people elected by the people to represent the popular vote of the people, except in a few states that is what they do. This means that the people actually do not decide who will win the election. How many people in each state electoral college is decided based on the population of the area they represent. So, their role is actually deciding who will win the Presidency and who will be Vice-President.

"In each presidential election year, a group of candidates for elector is nominated by political parties and other groupings in each state, usually at a state party convention, or by the party state committee. It is these elector-candidates, rather than the presidential and vice-presidential nominees, for whom the people vote in the November election, which is held on Tuesday after the first Monday in November. In most states, voters cast a single vote for the slate of electors pledged to the party presidential and vice-presidential candidates of their choice. The slate winning the most popular votes is elected; this is known as the winner-take-all, or general ticket, system.

Electors assemble in their respective states on Monday after the second Wednesday in December. They are pledged and expected, but not required, to vote for the candidates they represent. Separate ballots are cast for President and Vice President, after which the electoral college ceases to exist for another four years. The electoral vote results are counted and certified by a joint session of Congress, held on January 6 of the year succeeding the election. A majority of electoral votes (currently 270 of 538) is required to win. If no candidate receives a majority, then the President is elected by the House of Representatives, and the Vice President is elected by the Senate, a process known as contingent election" (History.com, 2010).

Taking a position on whether the electoral college should be abolished in favor of a direct popular vote

It is the opinion of this writer that the Electoral College should be taken out of the process in a Presidential Election. It is an antiquated system that was developed in the early stages of development of this country and the only way to truly update that part of the process would be to do away with it entirely and allow the people to truly decide who will run our country.

In today's society and current system of government, there is simply too much corruption taking place. If one watches the evening news it is easy to see that a good portion of the news will be updating the public on what has happened in the latest scandal, or corruption investigation. If it is well known that this level of corruption is taking place on a Federal level, how can anyone expect that same amount of corruption to not exist in the state levels that put the Federal level into office?

It is also well known that each politician has their own 'sponsors' or people that give them money in order to influence their decisions once in office. Some have even went as far as joking that politicians should wear patches on their clothes to show who is paying them just like NASCAR drivers have patches on their outfit to show who is paying for them to be there. If this is happening with virtually all politicians, how can anyone expect the ones elected to the electoral college to be any different? Who is there to safe guard the public's interest to ensure that the votes cast by the electoral college has not been influenced in the same manner?

"Presidential electors in contemporary elections are expected, and, in many cases pledged, to vote for the candidates of the party that nominated them. While there is evidence that the founders assumed the electors would be independent actors, weighing the merits of competing presidential candidates, they have been regarded as agents of the public will since the first decade under the Constitution. They are expected to vote for the presidential and vice-presidential candidates of the party that nominated them. Notwithstanding this expectation, individual electors have sometimes not honored their commitment, voting for a different candidate or candidates than the ones to whom they were pledged; they are known as "faithless" or "unfaithful" electors" (History.com, 2010).

Another reason for eliminating the electoral college is that it really does not represent the people and what they want. The Electoral College may seem like a fair system, but in fact it is not totally fair to the majority of the country. It does not truly represent the will of the people because it gives too much power to states with the most population. States that are less populated will have less of an opinion or vote in a Presidential election.

"There are over 300 million people in the United States, but just 538 people decide who will be president. In 2016, Hillary Clinton won the popular vote by more than one million votes, yet still lost the election on electoral votes. Even President-elect Donald Trump, who benefitted from the system, stated after the 2016 election that he believes presidents should be chosen by popular vote: "I would rather see it where you went with simple votes. You know, you get 100 million votes and somebody else gets 90 million votes and you win." Just as in 2000 when George W. Bush received fewer nationwide popular votes than Al Gore, Donald Trump will serve as the President of the United States despite being supported by fewer Americans than his opponent" (ProCon.org, 2017).

First Discussion Posting

1. Identify and describe three of the roles that a president must play during his or her tenure

    in office (for example, commander-in-chief).

"There is only one President of the United States. This one person must fill a number of

different roles at the same time. These roles are: (1) chief of state, (2) chief executive, (3) chief

administrator, (4) chief diplomat, (5) commander in chief, (6) chief legislator, (7) party chief,

and (8) chief citizen.

Chief of state refers to the President as the head of the government. He is the symbol of all the

people. In the United States, the President also rules over the government. In many countries, the

chief of state reigns over government but does not rule. Examples of this can be found in

England, Denmark, Japan, Italy, and Germany.

The President is also chief executive, vested by the Constitution with broad executive powers.

This power is used at home on domestic issues and also extends to foreign affairs. The executive

power is limited, however, by our government's system of checks and balances.

As chief administrator, the President is in charge of the executive branch of the federal

government. This branch employs more than 2.7 million civilians" (Pearsonschool, 2016).

2. Looking closely at the presidencies of George W. Bush and Barack Obama, provide one

    specific example from each man's presidency in which he fulfilled a role as president in a

    successful manner and one example where his effectiveness was an issue.

One of the instances where George W. Bush was successful was the no child left behind act. Even though I personally wonder how effective this program actually is at this time, it was a good idea and needs to be expanded upon. One instance where he was not successful was enacting the Patriot Act because this basically opened the door for authorities do abuse their power over the American People.

One instance where Barack Obama was successful is Obamacare as it is called in most conversations. I am one of the few people that would not be here alive at this moment if it were not for Obamacare. One instance where he was less than successful being when he failed to hold Wall Street and the major banks accountable for their actions against the economy.

Second Discussion Posting

"Prosecutors investigating the downing of flight MH17 over eastern Ukraine in 2014 said on Thursday they had identified the missile used to shoot down the plane as coming from Russia's armed forces.

Wilbert Paulissen, head of the crime squad of the Netherlands' national police, said the missile was fired from Russia's 53rd Anti-Aircraft Brigade.

"All the vehicles in a convoy carrying the missile were part of the Russian armed forces", he told a televised news conference.

Russia has denied involvement in the incident" (Reuters, 2018).

I chose this story because it is a perfect example of how the powers that be get away with murder, literally. This is one of the issues that our President should be making statements about and trying to hold Russia accountable for their actions. It is his role as chief diplomat to properly respond and hold Russia accountable.

Chapter Eight

Bureaucracy and You

1. What are the primary federal regulatory organizations responsible for food safety?

There are three main regulatory organizations within the federal government that are responsible for the safety of the food or food products consumed in America. These agencies are the Food Safety and Inspection Services also known as the FSIS. The second agency is the U.S. Food and Drug Administration also known as the FDA. The third agency is the Centers for Disease Control and Prevention also known as the CDC.

The FSIS is "the public health agency in the U.S. Department of Agriculture responsible for ensuring that the nation's commercial supply of meat, poultry, and egg products is safe, wholesome, and correctly labeled and packaged" (Foodsafety.gov, 2018).

The FSIS is governed by the U.S. Department of Agriculture. Their website can be found at https://www.fsis.usda.gov/wps/portal/fsis/home and their contact phone numbers for inquiries is (202) 720-9113. They can also be contacted via email at FSIS.Outreach@usda.gov and there are several other emails for various departments within the FSIS where contact can also be made.

They can also be contacted by postal mail at;

Headquarters:

Food Safety and Inspection Service

U.S. Department of Agriculture

1400 Independence Ave., S.W.

Washington, DC 20250-3700

Personnel/Human Resources:

FSIS Human Resources Office

Butler Square West 4th Floor

100 North Sixth Street

Minneapolis, MN 55403-1564

The FDA is "charged with protecting consumers against impure, unsafe, and fraudulently labeled products. FDA, through its Center for Food Safety and Applied Nutrition (CFSAN), regulates foods other than the meat, poultry, and egg products regulated by FSIS. FDA is also responsible for the safety of drugs, medical devices, biologics, animal feed and drugs, cosmetics, and radiation emitting devices" (Foodsafety.gov, 2018).

The FDA is also governed by the U.S. Department of Agriculture. Their website can be found at https://www.fda.gov/ and their contact phone number for inquiries is 1-888-463-6332. Their email address is a little more complicated because they simply provide a contact list based on their employee directory or their list of contacts based on region or state.

They too can also be contacted via postal mail at;

U.S. Food and Drug Administration

10903 New Hampshire Avenue

Silver Spring, MD 20993

The CDC "leads federal efforts to gather data on foodborne illnesses, investigate foodborne illnesses and outbreaks, and monitor the effectiveness of prevention and control efforts in reducing foodborne illnesses. CDC also plays a key role in building state and local health department epidemiology, laboratory, and environmental health capacity to support foodborne disease surveillance and outbreak response" (Foodsafety.gov, 2018).

It appears that the CDC is not governed by the U.S. Department of Agriculture but rather they partner with the Department of agriculture in many studies and research. Their website can be found at https://www.cdc.gov/ and their contact phone number is 1-800-232-4636. Their email address is not readily available but they do have a contact page where questions and inquiries can be sent to them and they will get back in touch with you. This contact page can be found at https://wwwn.cdc.gov/dcs/ContactUs/Form.

They can also be reached via postal mail at; 1600 Clifton Road Atlanta, GA 30329-4027 USA.

2. You are concerned that the eggs you bought at the grocery store might be contaminated. Which federal agency is responsible for ensuring the safety of eggs? Provide the agency name and a phone number or e-mail address for the agency.

The Food Safety and Inspection Service also known as the FSIS are the ones responsible for the safety of eggs in America today. The branch of that service that specifically handles poultry products is the National Advisory Committee on Meat and Poultry Inspection also known as the NACMPI.

"The major role of the Committee is to advise the Secretary of Agriculture on food safety policies that will contribute to USDA's regulatory policy development. The Committee will meet as a group on food safety concerns. Agency officials will present matters that are considered to be issues of concern with limited discussion taking place on the issue. The Committee would decide if further information is required on the issue, and if so, the Committee will assign the issue to a Sub-Committee for a thorough discussion and complete analysis of the issue, including recommendations" (USDA, 2018).

The phone number for the NACMPI is the same number as the FSIS (202) 720-9113. Their email address is broken down by agency and region. A full list of contacts can be found at https://www.fsis.usda.gov/wps/portal/informational/contactus.

3. You are concerned about the safety of some grapes you bought at the store. Which federal agency is responsible for the safety of produce? Provide the agency name and a phone number or e-mail address for the agency.

The federal agency responsible for the safety of grapes is the FDA also known as the Food and Drug Agency. "The Food and Drug Administration is responsible for protecting the public health by ensuring the safety, efficacy, and security of human and veterinary drugs, biological products, and medical devices; and by ensuring the safety of our nation's food supply, cosmetics, and products that emit radiation.

FDA also has responsibility for regulating the manufacturing, marketing, and distribution of tobacco products to protect the public health and to reduce tobacco use by minors.

FDA is responsible for advancing the public health by helping to speed innovations that make medical products more effective, safer, and more affordable and by helping the public get the accurate, science-based information they need to use medical products and foods to maintain and improve their health.

FDA also plays a significant role in the Nation's counterterrorism capability. FDA fulfills this responsibility by ensuring the security of the food supply and by fostering development of medical products to respond to deliberate and naturally emerging public health threats" (FDA, 2018).

The FDA can be contacted by phone at 1-888-463-6332 via the postal mail service at Food and Drug Administration

10903 New Hampshire Ave

Silver Spring, MD 20993

4. You are worried about the pesticides that farmers are using on crops they bring to the local farmers' market. Which federal agency would you contact to find out about the safety of pesticides used on local crops?

The federal agency that one would seek to contact about the use and safety of pesticides used on local crops would be the Environmental Protection Agency also known as the EPA.

"The mission of EPA is to protect human health and the environment.

EPA works to ensure that:

- Americans have clean air, land and water;

- National efforts to reduce environmental risks are based on the best available scientific information;

- Federal laws protecting human health and the environment are administered and enforced fairly, effectively and as Congress intended;

- Environmental stewardship is integral to U.S. policies concerning natural resources, human health, economic growth, energy, transportation, agriculture, industry, and international trade, and these factors are similarly considered in establishing environmental policy;

- All parts of society--communities, individuals, businesses, and state, local and tribal governments--have access to accurate information sufficient to effectively participate in managing human health and environmental risks;

- Contaminated lands and toxic sites are cleaned up by potentially responsible parties and revitalized; and

- Chemicals in the marketplace are reviewed for safety" (EPA, 2018).

The EPA can be contacted by phone according to one's region of the U.S. or via the National Response Center at 1-800-424-8802. Further contact information for each area of the U.S. can be found at https://www.epa.gov/home/forms/contact-epa.

First Discussion Posting

- How much should the power of elected officials be limited?

I believe that every power that elected officials have should be limited. There have simply been too many instances of elected officials abusing their position of power. Sometimes they have even went as far as using their position as an excuse to not act.

For example, many years ago I lived in a neighborhood that had a serious bird problem that was so bad the ground was covered in a new layer of bird feces every day. Every home in that neighborhood was a rental so the maintenance such as cleaning or bird removal had to be done by the property owners. After many efforts to get help forcing the property owners to act on the problem with no results, I contacted one of the state's representatives. The reply I got was that since I was not registered to vote, I was not one of the people that had any representation by their office. If I wanted to register to vote, then contact them again they would see if there was a problem.

If they think they are only there for registered voters instead of the public in general, or all citizens of their area then they should not be allowed to hold office in my opinion. This is how they can use their position of power to refuse to act.

"The noted German sociologist Max Weber (1864–1920) was the first scholar to systematically analyze the bureaucratic form of organization. Although Weber admired the bureaucratic form of organization for its efficiency, he recognized that its advantages carried a price. Bureaucrats' actions are dictated by position, specialty, and rule. In the process, they can become insensitive to circumstance. They often stick to the rules even when it's clear that bending them would produce a better result. "Specialists without spirit," was Weber's unflattering description of the bureaucratic mindset" (Patterson, 2017).

- Do you think civil service protections should be limited? For example, should elected officials have more power over hiring and firing?

Yes, I believe that civil service protections should be limited. Having those protections in place is one of the main reasons for the in-efficiency of the civil servant. How many people have been to the clerks' office to get a car title transferred in a large city and had to wait all day in line to do 10 minutes of paperwork, only to have to hear and sometimes watch them just standing around or talking to their friends on the phone instead of taking care of customers?

How long would it take you to get a pizza delivered if the delivery person knew they could not get fired whether or not they delivered the pizza? As to whether or not elected officials should have the power to hire or fire people in a civil service area, I believe if they did possess this power it should be very limited and only valid when other elected officials agreed. In this way it would be more of a checks and balances system. Elected officials need to be checked closer because they have a bad habit of selling out to the highest bidder or donators.

I live in an area that is very close to our state capitol and have seen with my own eyes how many civil service workers waste many hours a day just hanging out in the smoking area or walking around the block for exercise. If I had done this at my job when I was able to work I would have been fired on the spot, so I did not do it and was more productive. If those same civil servants had the same pressure, the bureaucracy

would run a lot smoother?

Several years ago, I took a friend of mine to the local food stamp office. She felt bad about having to get on food stamps so I went into the office with her to hopefully help her feel better about the process. After we and a full lobby of people had sat there for about an hour listening to the office workers through the thin walls talking and joking about their weekend plans and whether or not we had waited long enough, I decided to say something.

Since I felt I had heard enough of the rude office personnel talking bad about us and probably did not realize that we could all hear them, I thought they should know in a loud manner, just to make sure they heard me. But I did so in a polite manner so I would not go to jail. I simply told the woman at the front desk that I thought we had waited long enough to see someone especially since we all could hear what they were saying and I quoted some of them top prove I had heard them.

Needless to say, they got to work once I was done asking about how to file an official complaint in the state capitol. My friend was really embarrassed but relaxed a little when everyone else gave me a round of applause. BTW, yes, I am aware that they are no longer called food stamps.

Second Discussion

"Prosecutors agreed to drop one of two felony criminal cases against Missouri Gov. Eric Greitens after the governor's attorneys said he would resign if the allegations were dismissed, a spokeswoman for St. Louis' top prosecutor said Wednesday.

A day after Greitens announced that he would step down, St. Louis Circuit Attorney Kim Gardner said her office decided to dismiss a charge of computer data tampering following conversations with the defense team for the governor, who was once a rising star in the Republican Party.

"I remain confident we have the evidence required to pursue charges against Mr. Greitens, but sometimes pursuing charges is not the right thing to do for our city or our state," said Gardner, a Democrat" (Lieb & Salter, 2018).

In my opinion, this article is appalling and extremely dis-respectful to the American people. It goes to show how much unlimited power a politician or a prosecutor can have at any given moment. It is as if we are saying to people wanting to be a politician, if elected you cannot be committed of a crime. This needs to stop. Politicians need to be held to the same laws that the people they represent are forced to adhere to.

"A St. Louis judge approved the agreement, which has seven stipulations, two of which are sealed and unavailable to the public. One of the open stipulations states that Greitens has agreed to release Gardner and everyone in her office from civil liability.

The governor also was indicted on invasion-of-privacy charges in February in St. Louis for allegedly taking an unauthorized and compromising photo of a woman during an extramarital affair in 2015, before he was elected. The charge was dropped earlier this month, but a special prosecutor is considering whether to refile it.

The special prosecutor, Jean Peters Baker, said Tuesday that no deals have been made by her office with Greitens' attorneys" (Lieb & Salter, 2018).

If there was no deal made, then how was a judge able to approve the agreement? Are people so stupid that they cannot see there had to have been a deal made otherwise there would be no agreement for the judge to approve? Or do they think that we are so stupid that we would not notice?

Why do we not go to the jails of this country and tell prisoners that if you are a first-time offender and agree to never go back to your old job, your charges will be dropped? If we cannot hold politicians accountable for their actions, what is the point of holding anyone accountable for their actions?

We need a law that states if one holds any political office and are caught committing a crime, then the charges for that crime can never be dropped and they have to do the maximum amount of time for that crime. This would make politicians be more careful to NOT commit crimes against the people of this country. To do anything other than that is simply wasting time and money and the rights of the American people to be treated equally and fairly.

If we are going to do things like what is stated in this article, then we need to take the blindfold of the picture of lady justice while she is holding the scales of justice in all of this country's courtroom. Because she was not balancing the scales of equality in this situation and was definitely not blind to the fact that he is a politician that committed crimes against the American people.

Chapter Nine

Who Has the Power?

Of the president, Congress, and the Supreme Court, rank which you think has the most power, which has the second most, and which has the least.

"The Constitution of the United States divides the federal government into three branches to make sure no individual or group will have too much power:

- Legislative—Makes laws (Congress—House of Representatives and Senate)

- Executive—Carries out laws (President, Vice President, Cabinet, most federal agencies)

- Judicial—Evaluates laws (Supreme Court and other courts)

Each branch of government can change acts of the other branches:

- The President can veto legislation created by Congress and nominates heads of federal agencies.

- Congress confirms or rejects the President's nominees and can remove the President from office in exceptional circumstances.

- The Justices of the Supreme Court, who can overturn unconstitutional laws, are nominated by the President and confirmed by the Senate.

This ability of each branch to respond to the actions of the other branches is called the system of checks and balances" (USA.gov, 2018).

The founders of the United States Constitution were thinking about the future in the best manner they knew how to do when they designed the Constitution to ensure that no one power would be able to take complete control of the country. They had witnessed for themselves what could happen when one person or entity had complete control over a country. They wanted to ensure that the freedom of the people in this country would endure for eternity and have the power to adapt and overcome any obstacle that would attempt to take that freedom away from the people.

Therefore, trying to determine who has the most power is a difficult task. Congress has the power to make or change laws but only if they are unified. Since they are not unified most of the time, they limit their own power by arguing among themselves. Congress can change the judicial branch if they were unified. Congress can over-ride a decision of the President. If the President veto's their decision, they have the power to over-ride his veto.

The judicial branch has power but only to make decisions on cases that are presented to them. They cannot go find an issue and decide randomly. It has to be brought to them for a decision and even then, their hands are bound by the law as Congress has established them to be. Therefore, the judicial branch does have great power to change people's lives but it is limited in what issues that they are allowed to decide on.

The office of the President is the highest office or political position in the country. However even the President has to follow laws and procedures that are established by Congress. He does have the power to veto any decision that is made by Congress, but they can in return over-ride his veto by a 2/3 majority. In other words, only if they are unified do they possess this power over the President.

One of the fringe benefits that the office of the President does have is the power to pardon anyone at any time. The President even has the power to pardon himself before he is accused or convicted of a crime, or at least that is what we all have recently been told by the current President. However, the fact is "In a legal opinion issued just four days before Nixon stepped down, the Justice Department's Office of Legal Counsel concluded that a president can't pardon himself. The opinion was written in response to concerns that he might try to do so.

"Under the fundamental rule that no one may be a judge in his own case, the president cannot pardon himself," wrote Mary Lawton, who was then acting assistant attorney general" (Strohm & Pettypiece, 2018).

In conclusion of who has the most power, the answer would most definitely be Congress. They have the power to make and change the laws and procedures for every branch of the government because they are there to enforce the will of the people. But this power only exists if they are unified. Since they are not unified most of the time they limit themselves of power.

If you think that two or all three have equal amounts of power, explain why.

They all three absolutely do not have equal power. The Constitution designed the power to be checked and controlled by the other two branches. Thus, limiting and controlling the abuse of power by any one branch of the government.

Discuss limitations on the power of each branch of government.

"The framers of the Constitution sought a national government that could act decisively, but not one that would act irresponsibly. History had taught them to mistrust unrestricted majority rule. In times of stress or danger, popular majorities had often acted recklessly, trampling on the liberty of others. page 41Infact, liberty—the principle that individuals should be free to act and think as they choose, provided they do not infringe unreasonably on the freedom and well-being of others—was the governing ideal that the framers sought most to uphold. Americans enjoyed an unparalleled level of personal freedom as a result of their open society, and the framers were determined that it not be sacrificed to either European-style monarchy or mob-driven democracy. The threat to liberty was inherent in government because of its coercive power. Government's unique characteristic is that it alone can legally arrest, imprison, or even kill people who violate its directives. Force is not the only basis by which government maintains order, but without it, lawless individuals would prey on innocent people. The dilemma is that government itself can use force to intimidate or brutalize its opponents. "It is a melancholy reflection," James Madison wrote to Thomas Jefferson shortly after the Constitution's ratification, "that liberty should be equally exposed to danger whether the government has too much or too little power."" (Patterson, 2017).

The limitations are there to ensure that the power of one branch will not overcome the other two branches. The President's power is limited by the power of Congress and their ability to over-ride his decision. His power is also limited by the judicial system which as previously discussed has the power to control the President's power to pardon himself.

The power of Congress is limited by the power of the President to veto any of their decisions or laws they pass. Since they are usually not unified their power to over-ride his veto is limited by their own lack of unification. They can also be limited by the judicial branch by their interpretation of the laws passed by Congress. When Congress passes a law, it is then enforced and interpreted by the judicial branch.

The judicial branch is limited by Congress. Congress can either raise or lower the amount of chief justices that are on the Supreme Court. They are also limited by the fact that they are bound by law to strictly adhere to and enforce the laws of the land. They are limited in the issues they can decide about because they can only make decision on issues that are placed before them.

Conclusion

The branch that has the most power is Congress. The Office of the President comes in second in the race for power, and the judicial branch would place third in the race for power over the people. However, the power of Congress truly lies in the fact that it only fully exists when they are unified. If they are not unified and divided among themselves then they are simply limiting themselves to properly serve the people that elected them to office.

First Discussion

- Summarize a case and the final decision in 1–3 paragraphs.

The case I chose for this discussion is the case everyone has heard about lately and that is the cake shop in Colorado that decided they would not make a wedding cake for a gay couple. It is Docket #16-111.

The short version of this story is that there was a gay couple that wanted to get married even though their state did not approve of gay marriage at that time. They drove past several bakeries or cake shops and decided that they wanted this one shop and no others to make their wedding cake. The owner of the cake shop told them no because gay marriage was against his personal religious beliefs.

So, the gay couple sued the cake shop and the state of Colorado decided with the gay couple. The cake shop owner appealed the decision and took it to the U.S. Supreme Court. The U.S. Supreme Court recently decided that the cake shop owner did have the right to refuse to bake them a wedding cake. The cake shop owner offered to sell them other baked goods, but they did not want those items.

Personally, I believe that gay people have the right to get married and go through the trials and tribulations of marriage the same as anyone else. But they do not have the right to force everyone else to change their personal beliefs to suit a gay couple. Everyone has the right to their own personal religious belief without others trying to force them to change simply because they do not agree. If they could do that, then they could simply sue every Muslim religious organization in the U.S. and force them to accept gay couples.

- Discuss whether you think the current Supreme Court is conservative, liberal, or balanced. Use current Supreme Court decisions to argue your position.

I believe that the Supreme Court is close to liberal or balanced. The decision I mentioned in the first part of this discussion posting shows that they are somewhat liberal but balanced because they decision was a "7-to-2 decision was on the narrowest of grounds and left unresolved whether business owners have a free speech right to refuse to sell goods and services to same-sex couples" (Totenberg, 2018).

Their decision on May 21st that allowed companies to prevent employees from getting together on work related violations and allowing the company to force employees into individual arbitration also shows that they are balanced when making decision about employers and employees.

Second Discussion Posting

"President Trump is reportedly looking into using his pardon power in response to an expanding special counsel investigation of Russian influence in the 2016 election. If he really did pardon his aides, his family or himself to head off Robert Mueller's inquiry, the move probably would be constitutional but ultimately self-defeating for the president.

In using his power to pardon potential witnesses against him, Trump probably would convert a weak criminal investigation into a full-fledged impeachment effort. In 1833, Chief Justice John Marshall upheld a presidential pardon by Andrew Jackson by saying that a pardon is "an act of grace" by a president. A pardon in these circumstances would not be viewed as an act of grace, but a gratuity from an isolated president.

Trump clearly possesses the authority to pardon associates and family members under Article II, Section 2 of the U.S. Constitution, which states that the president "shall have power to grant reprieves and pardons for offenses against the United States, except in cases of impeachment." Although presidents have tended to wait for convictions before issuing pardons, Trump can do so in anticipation of federal charges. In Ex parte Garland in 1866, the Supreme Court ruled that the pardon power "may be exercised at any time after its commission, either before legal proceedings are taken, or during their pendency, or after conviction and judgment." That is precisely what Gerald Ford did when he pardoned Richard Nixon before any charges were brought against him" (Turley, 2017).

This is why the power of anyone in office should be more limited. I understand the process of the President showing compassion to people of this country. But when the people elect someone to that office, it is not so they can do whatever immoral or questionable act and then give themselves a pardon or pardon the people that got legally charged by doing illegal acts on behalf of the President. If we are going to allow anyone to do this to our country, then we should save some time and find a hardened criminal from the prison system and put them in that office

because we have basically done just that if we allow him to do whatever he pleases and then

pardon himself or his family. Seems like a conflict of interest to me but that is just my opinion.

References

Anderson, J., Riccardi, N., (2018), *Colorado Supreme Court knocks US Rep. Lamborn off ballot*

- ABC News. Retrieved from, http://abcnews.go.com/Politics/wireStory/colorado-

supreme-court-knocks-us-rep-lamborn-off-54675618

Apuzzo, M., (2018), *F.B.I. Raids Office of Trump's Longtime Lawyer Michael Cohen; Trump*

Calls It 'Disgraceful'. Retrieved from,

https://www.nytimes.com/2018/04/09/us/politics/fbi-raids-office-of-trumps-longtime-

lawyer-michael-cohen.html

Archives, (2016), *Constitutional Amendment Process | National Archives.* Retrieved from,

https://www.archives.gov/federal-register/constitution

Atwood, K., (2018), *Rex Tillerson warns of "growing crisis of integrity and ethics".* Retrieved

from, https://www.msn.com/en-us/news/politics/rex-tillerson-warns-of-growing-crisis-of-

integrity-and-ethics/ar-AAxnf16?OCID=ansmsnnews11

Blaszczak-Boxe, A., (2014), *Marijuana's History: How One Plant Spread Through the World.*

Retrieved from, https://www.livescience.com/48337-marijuana-history-how-cannabis-travelled-world.html

Borchardt, D., (2017), *Marijuana Sales Totaled $6.7 Billion In 2016*. Retrieved from, https://www.forbes.com/sites/debraborchardt/2017/01/03/marijuana-sales-totaled-6-7-billion-in-2016/#296df8d475e3

Buie, J., (2017), *Tennessee ranks last in voter turnout. How 2 lawmakers hope to change that.* Retrieved from, https://www.tennessean.com/story/news/2017/12/11/tennessee-voter-registration-cooper-dickerson-project-register/941325001/

Carpenter, M., (2017), *Advantages & Disadvantages of a Third Party*. Retrieved from, https://classroom.synonym.com/advantages-disadvantages-of-a-third-party-12083830.html

CCAGW, (2018), *Council for Citizens Against Government Waste - The Voter's Self Defense System - Vote Smart*. Retrieved from, https://votesmart.org/interest-group/13/council-for-citizens-against-government-waste#.WvMz-Jch3IU

Cooper, H., Gibbons-Neff, T., and Hubbard, B., (2018), *U.S., Britain and France Strike Syria Over Suspected Chemical Weapons Attack - The New York Times*. Retrieved from, https://www.nytimes.com/2018/04/13/world/middleeast/trump-strikes-syria-attack.html

Difference Between, (2018), *Difference between Articles of Confederation vs Constitution | Difference Between*. Retrieved from, http://www.differencebetween.net/language/difference-between-articles-of-confederation-vs-constitution/

DOJ, (2017), *History of Federal Voting Rights Laws | CRT | Department of Justice*. Retrieved from, https://www.justice.gov/crt/history-federal-voting-rights-laws

DPP, (2012), *Democratic Party on Abortion*. Retrieved from, http://www.ontheissues.org/celeb/Democratic_Party_Abortion.htm

Drugabuse, (2018), *DrugFacts: Marijuana | National Institute on Drug Abuse (NIDA)*. Retrieved from, https://www.drugabuse.gov/publications/drugfacts/marijuana

EPA, (2018), *Our Mission and What We Do | About EPA | US EPA*. Retrieved from, https://www.epa.gov/aboutepa/our-mission-and-what-we-do

FDA, (2018), *What We Do*. Retrieved from,

https://www.fda.gov/AboutFDA/WhatWeDo/default.htm

Foodsafety.gov, (2018), *Selected Federal Agencies with a Role in Food Safety | FoodSafety.gov*.

Retrieved from, https://www.foodsafety.gov/about/federal/index.html

Giffords, (2017), *Key Federal Acts Regulating Firearms | Giffords Law Center to Prevent Gun

Violence*. Retrieved from, http://lawcenter.giffords.org/gun-laws/federal-

law/background-resources/key-federal-acts-regulating-firearms/

Hartig, H., Perry, S., (2017), *Millennial poll: Strong majority want a third political party*.

Retrieved from, https://www.nbcnews.com/politics/politics-news/millennial-poll-strong-

majority-want-third-political-party-n824526

Henderson, A., (2017), *Disabled Kentuckians had lowest voter turnout for 2016 election*.

Retrieved from, https://www.courier-

journal.com/story/news/politics/2017/08/04/disability-voters-low-2016-election-

ky/484954001/

History, (2009), *Voting Rights Act of 1965 - Black History - HISTORY.com.* Retrieved from,

https://www.history.com/topics/black-history/voting-rights-act

History.com, (2010), *Electoral College - Facts & Summary - HISTORY.com.* Retrieved from,

https://www.history.com/topics/electoral-college

Jacques, R., (2017), *This Is Why Marijuana Should Be Legal Everywhere | HuffPost.* Retrieved

from, https://www.huffingtonpost.com/2013/10/24/marijuana-

legalization_n_4151423.html

Jamerson, J., (2018), *How Trump Unites and Divides the Parties - Washington Wire – WSJ.*

Retrieved from, https://blogs.wsj.com/washwire/2018/05/02/capital-journal-how-trump-

unites-and-divides-the-parties-rosensteins-rebuke-state-dept-felt-sidelined-by-tillerson/

Johnson, J., (2018), *'Worst Mistake I Ever Made': Union Support Nosedives as Workers Express

Regret for Trump Votes.* Retrieved from,

https://www.commondreams.org/news/2018/05/04/worst-mistake-i-ever-made-union-

support-nosedives-workers-express-regret-trump-votes

J.L.C., (2015), *What are the Three Branches of Government? | The Judicial Learning Center.*

Retrieved from, http://judiciallearningcenter.org/the-constitution/

Lieb, D., & Salter, J., (2018), *Prosecutor to drop felony charge against Missouri governor.*

Retrieved from, https://www.msn.com/en-us/news/us/prosecutor-to-drop-felony-charge-against-missouri-governor/ar-AAy1idN?OCID=ansmsnnews11

LPP, (2012), *Libertarian Party on VoteMatch.* Retrieved from,

http://www.ontheissues.org/Libertarian_Party_VoteMatch.htm

Madison, J. (1787). *Federalist no. 10: The union as a safeguard against domestic faction and insurrection.* Retrieved from:
https://www.congress.gov/resources/display/content/The+Federalist+Papers#TheFederalistPapers-10

Massie, T., (2018), *Meet Thomas | Congressman Thomas Massie.* Retrieved from,

https://massie.house.gov/about

Merriam-Webster, (2018), *The Electoral College | Definition of The Electoral College by Merriam-Webster*. Retrieved from, https://www.merriam-webster.com/dictionary/the%20Electoral%20College

McElwee, S., Schaffner, B., and Rhodes, J., (2017), *How Oregon Increased Voter Turnout More Than Any Other State*. Retrieved from, https://www.thenation.com/article/how-oregon-increased-voter-turnout-more-than-any-other-state/

Monk, L., (2013), *The Amendment Process | We the People | Constitution USA | PBS*. Retrieved from, http://www.pbs.org/tpt/constitution-usa-peter-sagal/we-the-people/amendment-process/

Mount, S. (2010). *Constitutional topic: due process*. Retrieved February 23, 2011 from //www.usconstitution.net/consttop_duep.html

Narconon, (2018), *Marijuana History*. Retrieved from, http://www.narconon.org/drug-information/marijuana-history.html

Patterson, T. (2017). *We The People: An Introduction to American Government, 12th Edition.*

[Bookshelf Online]. Retrieved from https://online.vitalsource.com/#/books/1260253481/

Persons, S., (2018), *Sheldon Adelson cuts $30 million check to House Republican group: Report - Washington Times*. Retrieved from,

https://www.washingtontimes.com/news/2018/may/10/sheldon-adelson-cuts-30-million-check-to-house-rep/

Pearsonschool, (2016), *The President's Job description*. Retrieved from,

https://assets.pearsonschool.com/asset_mgr/legacy/200938/section1_jobdescription_26523_1.pdf

ProCon.org, (2017), *The Electoral College: Top 3 Pros and Cons - ProCon.org*. Retrieved from,

https://www.procon.org/headline.php?headlineID=005330

Reuters, (2018), *Investigators say identify Russian military unit in MH17 downing*. Retrieved from, https://www.msn.com/en-us/news/world/investigators-say-identify-russian-military-unit-in-mh17-downing/ar-AAxJp1P?OCID=ansmsnnews11

Roberts, D., (2017), *Voting by mail is fair, safe, and easy. Why don't more states use it?*

Retrieved from, https://www.vox.com/policy-and-politics/2017/5/27/15701708/voting-by-mail

RPP, (2012), *Republican Party on Abortion.* Retrieved from,

http://www.ontheissues.org/celeb/Republican_Party_Abortion.htm

Serrano, A., (2018), *As Vets Demand Cannabis for PTSD, Science Races to Unlock Its Secrets – Scientific American.* Retrieved from, https://www.scientificamerican.com/article/as-vets-demand-cannabis-for-ptsd-science-races-to-unlock-its-secrets/

Strohm, C., & Pettypiece, S., (2018), *Can Trump Pardon Himself? Richard Nixon Was Told He Could Not – Bloomberg.* Retrieved from, https://www.bloomberg.com/news/articles/2018-06-04/trump-says-he-can-pardon-himself-nixon-was-told-he-couldn-t

Turley, J., (2017), *Yes, Trump can legally pardon himself or his family. No, he shouldn't. - The Washington Post.* Retrieved from, https://www.washingtonpost.com/outlook/yes-trump-can-legally-pardon-himself-or-his-family-no-he-shouldnt/2017/07/21/6134fb12-6e2d-11e7-b9e2-2056e768a7e5_story.html?noredirect=on&utm_term=.b066d7aac83f

Totenberg, N., (2018), *Supreme Court Decides In Favor Of Baker Over Same-Sex Couple In Cake-Shop Case: NPR*. Retrieved from,

https://www.npr.org/2018/06/04/605003519/supreme-court-decides-in-favor-of-baker-over-same-sex-couple-in-cake-shop-case

USA.gov, (2018), *Branches of the U.S. Government | USAGov*. Retrieved from,

https://www.usa.gov/branches-of-government

USDA, (2018), *NACMPI Committee Responsibilities*. Retrieved from,

https://www.fsis.usda.gov/wps/portal/informational/aboutfsis/!ut/p/a1/tVLLboMwEPyWHDgir8UjcEyRQqESKE3aBi6RAZs6woaAG7X9-ppUUU9pGon6sl5rdnY8GpSjLcolOfKaKN5K0ox97u5gBS72A4hTHy8hSp5X6UMQQJjaGpCNgAtnAdfmX1CO8lKqTr2ijA18MMtWKiqVAVzXXlJ9E4RLA1Tb8XIwoKf1W3MSqBtSHfnQ9h96TAiuFKX6UZJSdPxcxw0dqWlFB17LU1fyCmWWU_gFwdj0rao0bQt7pk8q16SMMp9V4BLGvvX98oXQOQMuW5Bpj-Y_DOEjYIiW6w0OnTscWTZa3yjqCqE7NaEzNeF8YsL4dg_jPySb7w-HfKHzOUbyXaHtPwW0E0_C27Pu_nPDhNgliUkKDyynqWezL2fV0Gs!/?1dmy¤t=true&urile=wcm%3apath%3a%2Ffsis-content%2Finternet%2Fmain%2Ftopics%2Fregulations%2Fadvisory-committees%2Fnacmpi%2Fnacmpi-responsibilities

Walsh, K., (2015), *Voting Rights Still a Political Issue, 50 Years Later | Politics | US News*.

Retrieved from, https://www.usnews.com/news/articles/2015/08/04/voting-rights-still-a-political-issue-50-years-later

Wyman, K., (2008), *Washington's voter turnout breaks record - News Release - News Room –*

WA Secretary of State. Retrieved from, https://www.sos.wa.gov/office/news-releases.aspx#/news/762

www.ingramcontent.com/pod-product-compliance
Lightning Source LLC
Chambersburg PA
CBHW050047260726
48658CB00005B/1822